Does a Bear Wear a Hat in the Winter?

BY LESLIE FALCONER AND KELLY NOGOSKI   ILLUSTRATED BY KELLY NOGOSKI

First published by Experience Early Learning Company
7243 Scotchwood Lane, Grawn, Michigan 49637 USA

Text Copyright © 2014 by Experience Early Learning Co.
Manufactured in No.8, Yin Li Street, Tian He District, Guangzhou, Guangdong,
China by Sun Fly Printing Limited
4th Printing 01/2023

ISBN: 978-1-937954-16-1
Visit us at www.ExperienceEarlyLearning.com

Does a bear wear a hat to keep warm in the winter?

A bear uses his **fur** to keep warm in the winter.

Does a rabbit wear boots to jump in the snow?

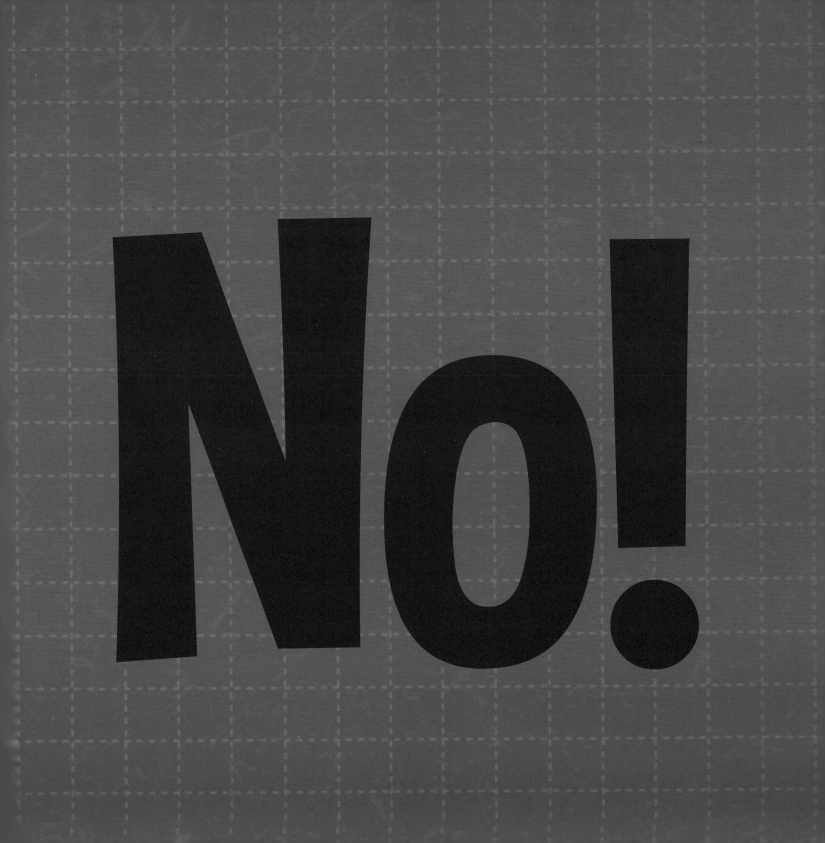

A rabbit uses his large feet to hop over the snow.

Does a frog need an umbrella in the rain?

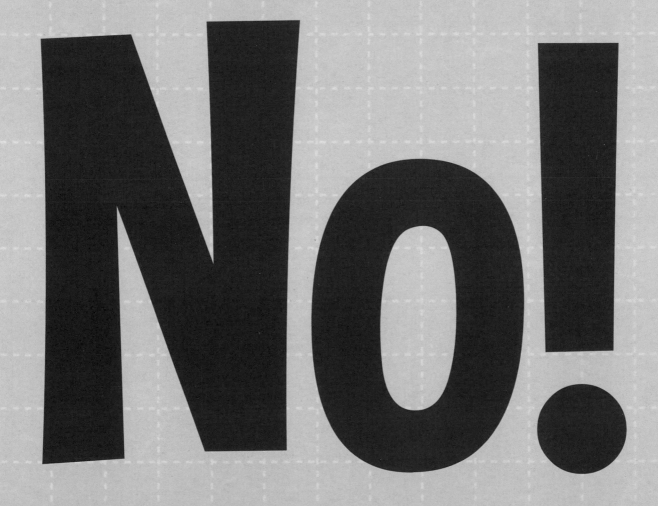

A frog likes to get wet and even drinks through his skin.

Does a duck need
a raincoat to keep
dry in the rain?

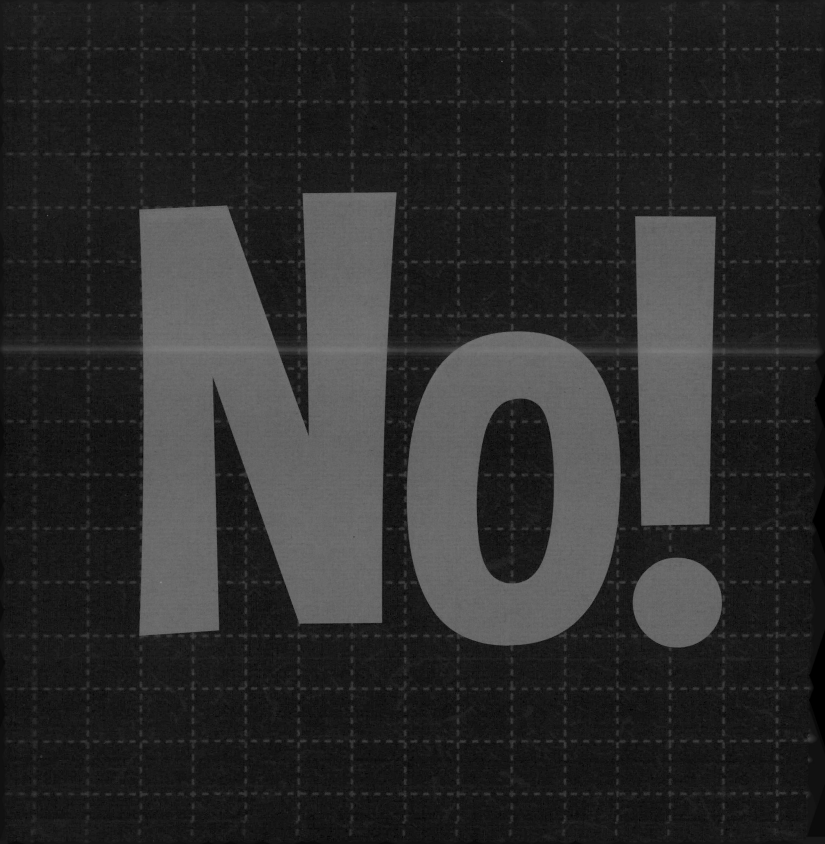

A duck's feathers repel water and keep him warm and dry.

Does a turtle wear sunscreen to protect his skin from the sun's rays?

A turtle's shell protects his skin from the sun.

Does a fish need a swimsuit to swim in the water?

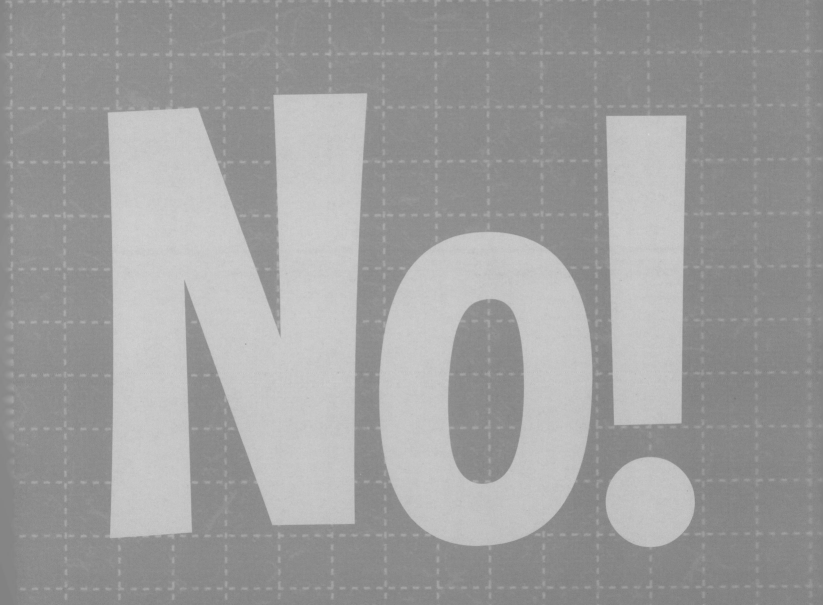

A fish's scales help him move through the water.

Does a chipmunk need a bag to carry the nuts he harvests?

A chipmunk uses his cheeks to store food he finds.

Does a crane need an airplane to migrate?

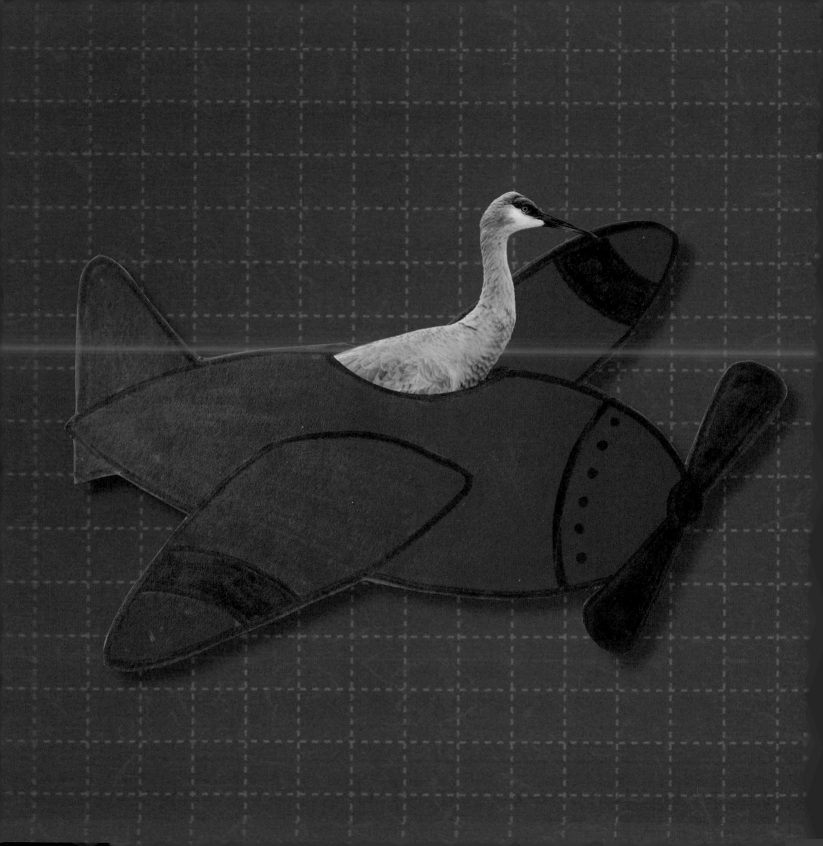

A crane uses his **wings** to migrate.

Do you think a

bear, rabbit, frog, duck,

turtle, fish, chipmunk and crane

are made perfectly for
the weather where they live?